What Are Elections?

by Jennifer Boothroyd

Lerner Publications ◆ Minneapolis

LERNER

SOURCE

Expand learning beyond the printed book. Download free, complementary educational resources for this book from our website, www.lerneresource.com.

The images in this book are used with the permission of: © Rob Crandall/Alamy, p. 4; © Blend Images - Hill Street Studios/agency/Getty Images, pp. 5, 15, 16; © BobSmithImages/Alamy, p. 6; © Jessica McGowan/Getty Images, p. 7; © Bill Clark/CQ Roll Call/Getty Images, pp. 8, 9, 14; © Michael Bryant-Pool/Getty Images, p. 10; © Alex Wong/Getty Images, p. 11; © Daniel Acker/Bloomberg/Getty Images, p. 12; © iStockphoto.com/PeopleImages, p. 13; © iStockphoto.com/YinYang, p. 17; © Gabriel Bouys/AFP/Getty Images, p. 18; © Chip Somodevilla/Getty Images, p. 19; © Win McNamee/Getty Images, p. 20; © iStockphoto.com/Jacek_Sopotnicki, p. 21; © Ariel Skelley/Blend Images /Getty Images, p. 22. Front cover: © iStockphoto.com/YinYang.

Main body text set in ITC Avant Garde Gothic Std Medium 21/25.
Typeface provided by Adobe Systems.

Lerner Publications Company
A division of Lerner Publishing Group, Inc.
241 First Avenue North
Minneapolis, MN 55401 USA

For reading levels and more information, look up this title at www.lernerbooks.com.

Library of Congress Cataloging-in-Publication Data

Boothroyd, Jennifer, 1972–
    What are elections? / by Jennifer Boothroyd.
      pages cm. — (First step nonfiction. Exploring government)
    Includes index.
    ISBN 978-1-4677-8576-1 (lb : alk. paper)—ISBN 978-1-4677-8615-7 (pb : alk. paper)—
ISBN 978-1-4677-8616-4 (eb pdf)
    1. Elections—United States—Juvenile literature. I. Title.
JK1978.B66 2016
324.60973—dc23
                                      2015000303

Manufactured in the United States of America
1 – CG – 7/15/15

Table of Contents

Election Day

It's **Election** Day!

Many elections happen in November.

On Election Day, people **vote**.

When people vote, they make a choice.

A town leader greets voters.

They choose our leaders.

The leaders will run our **government**.

A person who wants to be a government leader is a **candidate**.

Candidates ask **citizens** to vote for them.

Candidates give speeches.

Candidates talk to voters.

Voters learn about the candidates.

People vote for different candidates.

The voters decide who will do the best job.

Time to Choose

In the United States, you must be 18 years old to vote.

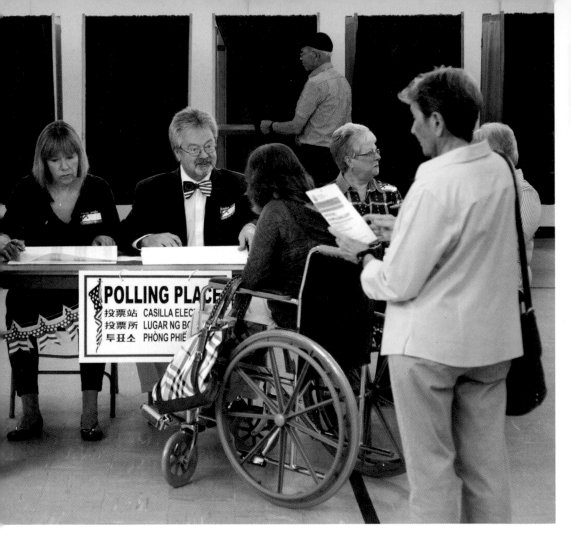

People can vote in person
or by mail.

Voters mark their choices on **ballots**.

People count the votes.

The candidate with the most votes wins the election.

Some of the leaders we choose make new laws.

Good laws can make our country better.

When we vote, we help
lead our country.

Glossary

ballots – the pieces of paper that people use to vote

candidate – a person who wants to be an elected leader

citizens – people who live in a country and have rights in that country

election – an organized vote

government – the people in charge of a city, a state, or a country

vote – to make a choice in an election

Index